Frida Kahlo

Frida Kahlo

The Artist in the Blue House

Prestel
Munich · London · New York

What a proud looking woman!

But she also seems a bit serious, with her hair pulled up and wound into a turban. Even her eyebrows, which meet in the middle, make her appear rather stern. But look more closely ... those same eyebrows resemble a bird in flight! In fact, birds are everywhere in this picture. Two brightly-colored parrots are perching happily on the woman's shoulders and two more are sitting in her lap.

Who could this woman be?
Where does she come from?
Who painted her?

The woman in the picture painted her own portrait.
Her name is **Frida Kahlo** and she lived in Mexico.

Me and My Parrots, 1941

2

In her paintings, the artist tells the story of her life.

Frida Kahlo aged 5 (front left) with her sisters and other relatives, 1912

Guillermo Kahlo and Matilde Calderón on their wedding day, photograph, 1898

The photo above shows Frida with other members of her family taken in her parents' garden when she was a little girl.

In the painting opposite, the red ribbon in her hand leads to her grandparents. Frida's mother's parents (top left) were Mexican and her father's parents (top right) came from Europe. They look very different, don't they? In the middle of the picture, Frida painted her parents on their wedding day. Little Frida is already in her mother's womb.

My Grandparents, My Parents, and I, 1936

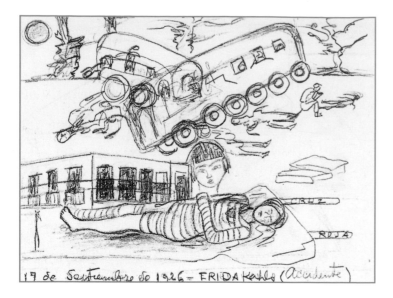

Accident, 1926

When Frida was eighteen years old, she was in a terrible accident. The bus she was traveling on ran into a streetcar, and Frida was badly injured. In this pencil sketch she made a year later, the crash can be clearly seen. Frida is lying on a stretcher, all bound up in bandages.

The accident completely changed her life, forcing her to spend months in bed. It was during that time that she started painting to help deal with the pain and the boredom. Even years later, Frida often had to paint lying down in bed because she was too ill to sit up.

Can you see who the people are in this painting?

They are the artist's parents and grandparents.

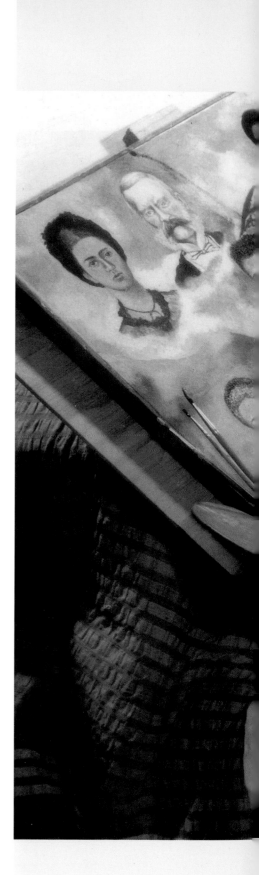

Frida Kahlo painting in bed, 1952

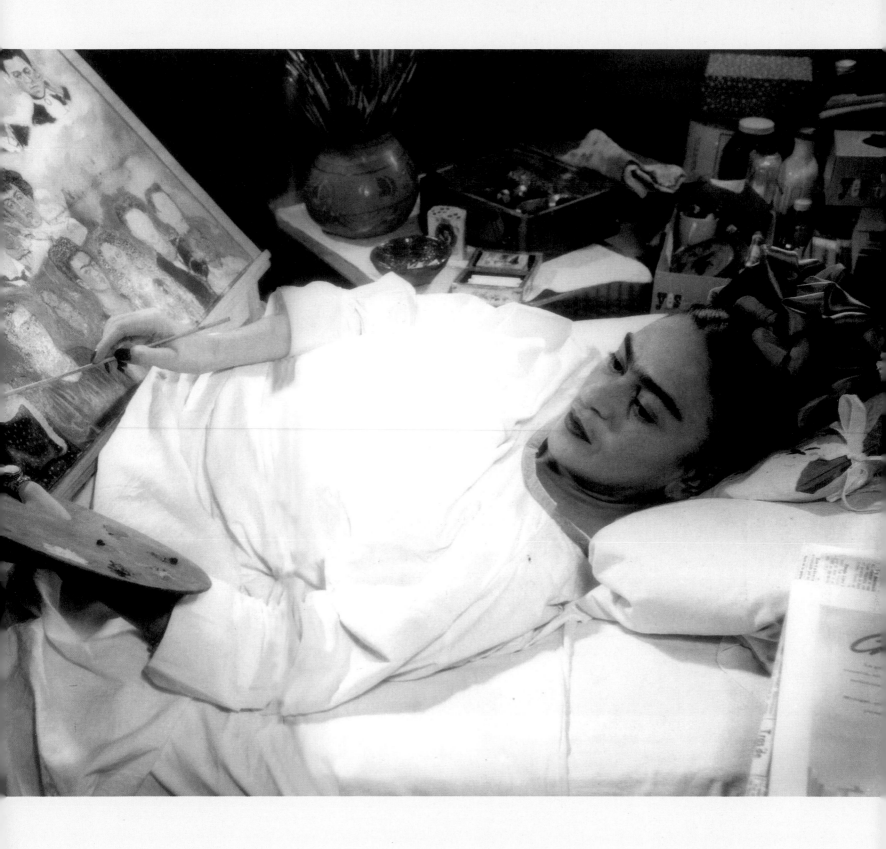

In this picture Frida looks like an exotic princess. She is wearing the traditional costume of the Tehuana, a proud and confident people who lived in Mexico for many centuries. Frida always liked to dress up. As a young girl she often wore men's suits, and when she was older she dressed like a Tehuana woman. Lace frames her beautiful but serious face; and on her forehead, directly above her curved eyebrows, is the face of a man.

Frida in the traditional costume of a Tehuana woman in front of her collection of ethnic Mexican ceramic ware, 1942

His name is **Diego Rivera** and he was also a famous Mexican painter.

But why did Frida paint him as if he were inside her own head?

Self Portrait as Tehuana Woman, 1943

Frida and Diego, 1928

Frida and Diego, 1930

Diego Rivera and Frida Kahlo met because Frida wanted to show the well-known artist her paintings and find out what he thought of them. Diego felt that she was a very talented painter.

Frida and Diego soon fell in love and married—in fact, Frida painted this picture (opposite) from a wedding photo. She seems so small and delicate next to such a big man, and her tiny feet hardly seem to touch the ground.

Looking at this painting, it is easy to understand why the couple were sometimes called

the dove and the elephant!

Frida admired Diego both as a person and an artist, as this picture of Diego holding an artist's seems to show. He was the great love of her life and can be seen in many of her paintings.

Frida and Diego Rivera, 1931

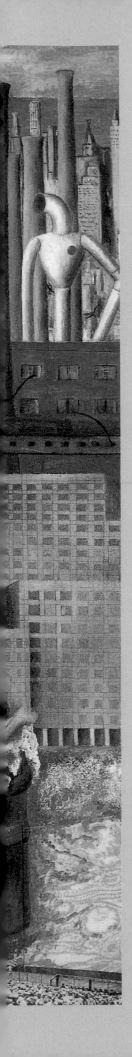

There is so much to discover in this picture ...

... skyscrapers and factories, old buildings, a temple and a church, an

overflowing bin, a telephone, a beautiful woman, a burning house, and

a crowd of people. Can you tell where this is? Right in the background,

on the horizon, you can see the Statue of Liberty, which is in New York.

When she painted this picture, Frida was no longer in Mexico but had gone

north with Diego to live in the United States. It shows how she saw the

United States and how homesick she was during her stay there.

This picture was made using a technique known as "collage."

Frida took lots of little pictures and joined them together—like puzzle

pieces—to make one big picture. Some of the pieces are painted,

whereas others have been cut out and pasted in.

My Dress is Hanging There, 1933

Diego and Frida lived in the United States for three years.

Here she has painted herself on the border between Mexico and the United States.

These two countries were contrasting worlds for her. On the right there are skyscrapers

and factories; the American flag almost disappears in a cloud of smoke billowing out of

the factory chimney stacks. To the left of Frida there are ancient temples, mysterious

sculptures, and colorful Mexican plants. If you look closely, it is quite clear which of

these two worlds Frida felt she belonged to best.

Frida with Mexican sculptures, 1952/53

In this photo, as in the painting, Frida is

wearing a magnificent dress and is sitting

in front of ancient sculptures of Mexican

folk art. This was the culture of her homeland

which she longed for during her years in the

United States.

Self Portrait on the Border between Mexico and the United States, 1932

What a mysterious picture!

Frida painted herself holding her husband, Diego, in her arms, making him look like a child who needs to be protected. Frida herself is embraced by a large, greenish woman made of stone. This figure is Mother Earth, from whose body the trees and plants of Mexico grow. A mysterious creature with two strong arms clasps the earth. This is the universe, which links day and night—letting the sun and the moon shine at the same time.

In the living room, 1940

Frida painted the world the way it used to be shown in old Mexican legends. In the front of the painting, lying on the dark arm of the universe, is Frida's favorite dog, fast asleep on a bed of leaves. The dog's name was Mr. Xólotl—which may seem strange to us, but Xólotl was the name of a dog-headed god in ancient Mexico. As the story goes, Xólotl helped carry the dying across the wide river dividing the land of the living from the land of the dead, and he stayed to watch over them when they were on the other side.

The Embrace of Love of the Universe, the Earth (Mexico), I, Diego, and Mr. Xólotl, 1949

The painting shown at left is just as mysterious. A pretty, young Mexican girl called **Lucha Maria** is sitting all alone in a big, wide, open space, holding a brightly-colored toy airplane in her hand. But take a closer look and you will see something else! On the horizon, above the temples in which the Aztecs—the people of ancient Mexico—once worshipped their powerful gods, both the sun and the moon are shining at the same time. Here, as in many of Frida's paintings, the artist likes to tell stories about the history of her homeland. For the Aztecs, the sun and the moon, light and dark, and life and death all help to keep the world turning.

Roots, 1943

Is this a person or a plant?

Frida is lying stretched out on a wide, open plain where nothing seems to grow. The soil is dry and cracked. It seems impossible for anything to live here. But how strange: there are beautiful green branches and leaves growing through a hole in her chest, as if she is giving life to these plants herself. The artist was close to nature—and felt firmly rooted in the soil of her homeland.

Who is in the picture with the red background?

Is there just one person or are there two? Perhaps you have already solved

the riddle—the right half of the face is Frida's and the left half is that of

her husband, Diego. Cover up the left side and look how sad and serious

Frida seems. Now cover up the other side—Diego looks happy and contented,

rather like the red sun in the painting below, which is giving life and warmth

to the plants that grow around it.

The Sun and Life, 1947

Double Portrait, Diego and I, 1944

Now here's a strange creature: half human, half animal.

The stag has Frida's head, and magnficent antlers are growing through her hair!

But the animal's body has lots of arrows sticking in it and it is bleeding.

Frida's pictures often tell of the pain she suffered as a result of her accident.

Painting gave her strength and the will to live. This is exactly what she is saying in the stag picture, too. Although the animal is hurt and injured, it is proudly holding its head high as it leaps through the forest.

Frida Kahlo with her pet deer, Granizo, 1939

To paint the animal's body, Frida used her pet deer, Granizo, as a model. She loved her pets more than anything else, and she gathered them around her whenever she felt lonely.

Wounded Stag, 1946

Frida's Diary

Frida began to keep a diary when she was thirty-five years old, and she would continue to do so for the rest of her life. She not only jotted down what she did every day, but also wrote about all her feelings, her fears, and her hopes. The artist's diary tells us a lot about her life and the way she thought. She recorded her thoughts in drawings, watercolors, stories, and poems.

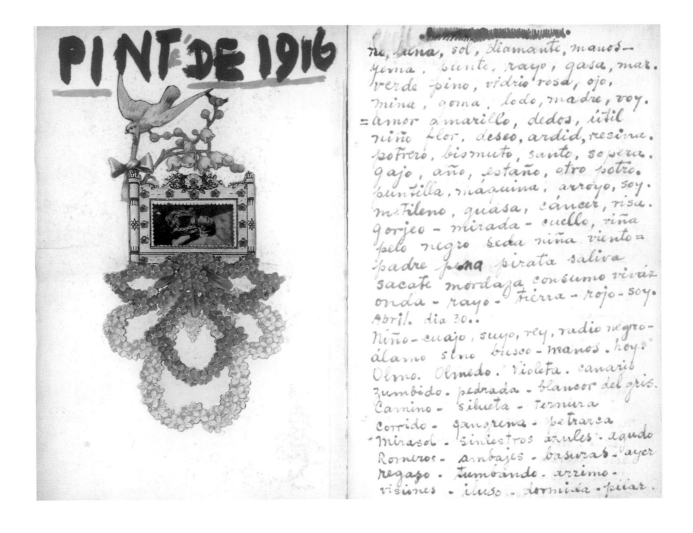

"**Luna**" and "**Sol**" are Spanish for "moon" and "sun"—and these are the words that Frida wrote in the sky above the old temple. Can you think of any other pictures in which the sun and the moon can be seen at the same time? "**Yo,**" which means "me," is written below the woman, whose face we cannot see properly, pictured here all alone. She is wearing the traditional, lacey dress worn by the Tehuana women that Frida liked to wear so much.

The artist's life was linked very closely to the old gods and the sagas of her Mexican homeland.

Frida painted a portrait next to the horse called "The Jealous Woman." What do you think could have made her turn green with jealousy?

These two pages from Frida's diary are dedicated to Diego. **"My Diego. I am not alone,"** she wrote next to the brightly-colored drawing.

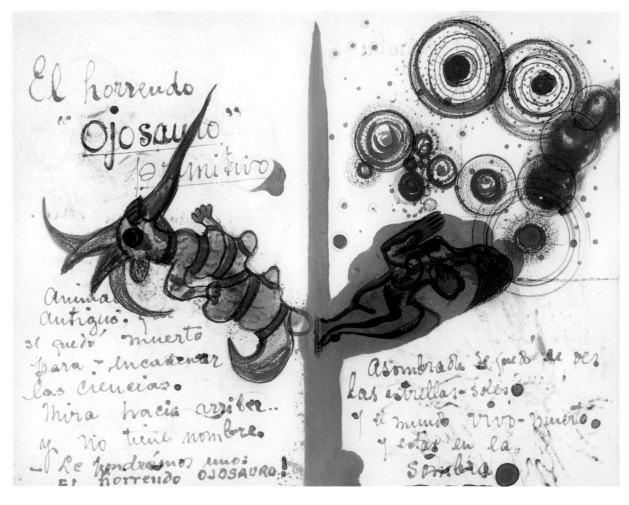

Frida drew a frightening, one-eyed monster opposite a woman looking at the stars.

"Real World" is the translation of the words above the angels and the bird;

"Sundance" was the name Frida gave to the animals having fun above on

the right. We can also see some of the Mexican gods dancing. Can you find them?

Frida's Life

Magdalena Carmen Frida Kahlo y Calderón was born in Coyoacán, a suburb of Mexico City, on July 6, 1907. Frida had one younger sister and two older sisters. Matilde, Adriana, Frida, and Cristina grew up in "The Blue House" in Coyoacán. When

"The Blue House," Frida Kahlo's home in a suburb of Mexico City is now a museum called the Museo Frida Kahlo "Casa Azul".

she was six years old, Frida became ill with polio. It left her with one leg shorter than the other, and she later tried to hide this by wearing long skirts. Frida was a very intelligent girl who did well in school and had hoped to study medicine one day. She was among the first women to attend one of Mexico's top schools, where only men had been allowed to study up until that time.

But in 1925, something happened that changed her life. Frida had a terrible accident in which she injured her back badly and broke several bones. She had to spend many months in bed. During this time she started to paint to pass the time and to take her mind off the pain. A big mirror was hung over her bed so that she could paint pictures of herself. Although Frida had many operations,

they did not really help her; and she suffered for the rest of her life because of the crash.

By the time she met Diego Rivera, who was twenty years older than her and already a famous artist, Frida had recovered enough to lead a more or less normal life. Frida showed him her pictures and he was very impressed by this young woman and her talent. Diego and Frida fell in love and married in 1929. Although they very much wanted to have children, Frida could not have any.

In 1930, Diego and Frida moved to the United States where Diego had been asked to paint some large murals. Frida never enjoyed living there and was always homesick.

Frida Kahlo in her bedroom, 1953

They returned to Mexico in 1933.

Frida and Diego argued a lot and divorced at the end of 1939. But one year later, in San Francisco, they married each other again!

In 1941, Frida's father died. Diego

and Frida moved into the house where she was born: "The Blue House" in Coyoacán.

Frida began teaching at an art school. Because of her poor health, she soon found she could not travel to the school, so the other students came to her home instead.

In 1950, Frida had seven separate operations on her spine, but they did not make her feel better. She had to spend most of her time in a wheelchair and was often too weak to paint.

In 1953, the first show of her paintings was held in Mexico. Although she was very ill, she was wheeled to the show's opening in her bed. A year later, Frida caught pneumonia and died on July 13. Hundreds of people

came to her funeral.

Frida Kahlo has since become a very famous artist. Her home, "The Blue House" in Coyoacán, was opened as a museum in 1958.

The pictures in this book

front cover:
Self Portrait with Monkey, 1938
Oil on masonite, 40 x 30 cm. Albright
Knox Gallery, Buffalo. Bequest of
A. Conger Goodyear, 1966

Title page:
Frida Kahlo, photographed by Nickolas
Muray, 1938/39. International Museum
of Photography, George Eastman House,
Rochester, New York (photo: courtesy
George Eastman House)

page 3
Me and My Parrots, 1941 (detail)
Oil on canvas, 82 x 63 cm. Collection
of Mr. and Mrs. Harold H. Steam,
New Orleans

page 4
My Grandparents, My Parents, and I, 1936
Oil and tempera on metal, 31 x 34 cm.
The Museum of Modern Art, New York.
Gift of Allan Roos, M.D., and B. Matheu
Roos (photo: Scala)

page 5
Guillermo Kahlo and Matilde Calderón on
their wedding day, photograph, 1898

Frida Kahlo aged 5 (*front left*) with her
sisters and other relatives, photographed
by Guillermo Kahlo, 1912
Cristina Kahlo, Mexico City

page 6
Accident, 1926
Pencil on paper. 20 x 27 cm
Coronel Collection, Cuernavaca/Morelos
(photo: Rafael Doniz)

pages 6/7
Frida Kahlo painting a picture of her
family, photographed by Juan Gunzmán,
1952, Achivo CENIDIAP-INBA, Mexico City

page 8
Self Portrait as Tehuana Woman or Diego in My Thoughts or
Thoughts about Diego, 1943
Oil on board, 76 x 61 cm. Jacques and
Natasha Gelman Collection, Mexico City
(photo: Rafael Doniz)

page 9
Frida Kahlo in the traditional costume of a
Tehuana woman in front of her collection of
ethnic Mexican ceramic ware, photographed
by Bernhard G. Silberstein, 1942

page 10
Frida and Diego, photograph, 1928
Frida and Diego, photograph, 1930

page 11
Frida and Diego Rivera or *Frida Kahlo and Diego Rivera*,
1931
Oil on canvas, 100 x 79 cm. San Francisco
Museum of Modern Art. Albert M. Bender
Collection, gift of Albert M. Bender

page 12
My Dress is Hanging There or *New York*, 1933
Oil and collage on board, 46 x 50 cm
Private collection

page 14
Frida with Mexican sculpture, photographed
by Antonio Kahlo, 1952/53
(photo: Rafael Doniz)

page 15
*Self Portrait on the Border between Mexico and
the United States*, 1932
Oil on metal, 31 x 35 cm
Private collection, New York

page 16
Frida Kahlo in her living room, photographed
by Bernard G. Silberstein, 1940

page 17
*The Embrace of Love of the Universe, the Earth (Mexico),
I, Diego, and Mr. Xóloti*, 1949
Oil on canvas, 70 x 60.5 cm
Private collection, Mexico City
(photo: Rafael Doniz)

page 18
Lucha Maria, the Girl from Tehuacan, 1942
Oil on board, 54.5 x 43 cm
Private collection, Mexico
(photo: Rafael Doniz)

page 19
Roots or *The Pedregal*, 1943
Oil on metal, 30.5 x 50 cm
Private collection, Houston, Texas
(photo: akg Images, Berlin)

page 20
The Sun and Life, 1947
Oil on board, 40 x 50 cm
Private collection, Mexico City
(photo: Rafael Doniz)

page 21
Double Portrait, Diego and I (II) or *Diego and Frida
1929–1944 (II)*, 1944
Oil on board, 13.5 x 8.5 cm
Private collection, Mexico City
(photo: Rafael Doniz)

page 22
Frida Kahlo with her pet deer, Granizo,
photographed by Nickolas Muray, 1939
International Museum of Photography,
George Eastman House, Rochester, NY
(photo: courtesy George Eastman House)

page 23
Wounded Stag or *The Little Stag* or
I am a Poor Little Deer, 1946
Oil on board, 22.4 x 30 cm
Private collection, Houston, Texas
(photo: Rafael Doniz)

pages 24–27
Pages from Frida Kahlo's diary, Museum
Rivera/Kahlo, Mexico (Frida Kahlo:
Gemaltes Tagebuch, facsimile with com-
mentary by Sarah M. Lowe, Munich 1995)

page 28
"The Blue House", photograph

Frida Kahlo in her bedroom, photographed
by Lola Alvarez Bravo, 1953

Lola Alvarez Bravo, Galéria Juan Martin,
Mexico City

back cover:
Lucha Maria, the Girl from Tehuacan, 1942
(see page 18)

Text and picture selection by Magdalena Holzhey

The Library of Congress Cataloguing-in-Publication data is available.
The Deutsche Bibliothek holds a record of this publication in the
Deutsche Nationalbibliografie; detailed bibliographical data can be
found under: http://dnb.ddb.de
The title and concept of the "Adventures in Art" series and the
titles and design of its individual volumes are protected by copyright
and may not be copied or imitated in any way.

© Prestel Verlag, Munich · London · New York, 2003;
revised edition 2015

© for the artworks: Banco de México Diego Rivera Frida Kahlo
Museums Trust / VG-Bild-Kunst, Bonn 2015;
© Lola Alvarez Bravo: VG Bild-Kunst, Bonn 2015

Prestel Verlag, Munich
Prestel, a member of Verlagsgruppe Random House GmbH

www.prestel.de

Prestel Publishing Ltd.
14-17 Wells Street
London W1T 3PD

Prestel Publishing
900 Broadway, Suite 603,
New York, NY 10003

www.prestel.com

Prestel books are available worldwide. Please contact your nearest
bookseller or one of the above addresses for information concerning
your local distributor.

Translated from the German by Ishbel Flett, Edinburgh
Edited by Christopher Wynne and Brad Finger
Design and layout: WIGEL, Munich
Originations: ReproLine, Munich
Printing: Printer Trento, Trento

Verlagsgruppe Random House FSC®N001967
The FSC®-certified paper Hello Fat matt has been
produced by Condat, Le Lardin Saint-Lazare, France.

ISBN 978-3-7913-7229-7